I LIKE JACK RUSSELL TERRIERS!

Linda Bozzo

DISCOVER DOGS WITH THE AMERICAN CANINE ASSOCIATION

AMERICAN CANINE ASSOCIATION, INC.
America's Largest Veterinary Health Tracking Canine Registry
OFFICIAL SEAL
ACA

It is the mission of the American Canine Association (ACA) to provide registered dog owners with the educational support needed for raising, training, showing, and breeding the healthiest pets expected by responsible pet owners throughout the world. Through our activities and services, we encourage and support the dog world in order to promote best-known husbandry standards as well as to ensure that the voice and needs of our customers are quickly and properly addressed.

Our continued support, commitment, and direction are guided by our customers, including veterinary, legal, and legislative advisors. ACA aims to provide the most efficient, cooperative, and courteous service to our customers and strives to set the standard for education and problem solving for all who depend on our services.

For more information, please visit www.acacanines.com, email customerservice@acadogs.com, phone 1-800-651-8332, or write to the American Canine Association at PO Box 121107, Clermont, FL 34712.

Published in 2018 by Enslow Publishing, LLC.
101 W. 23rd Street, Suite 240, New York, NY 10011

Library of Congress Cataloging-in-Publication Data

Names: Bozzo, Linda, author.
Title: I like Jack Russell terriers! / Linda Bozzo.
Description: New York : Enslow Publishing, 2018. | Series: Discover dogs with the American Canine Association | Includes bibliographical references and index. | Audience: Grades K to 3.
Identifiers: LCCN 2017001307 | ISBN 9780766086449 (library-bound) | ISBN 9780766088764 (pbk.) | ISBN 9780766088702 (6-pack)
Subjects: LCSH: Jack Russell terrier—Juvenile literature.
Classification: LCC SF429.J27 B69 2017 | DDC 636.755—dc23
LC record available at https://lccn.loc.gov/2017001307

Printed in the United States of America

Photo Credits: Cover, p. 1 Eric Isselee/Shutterstock.com; p. 3 (left) Andreina Nunez/Shutterstock.com; p. 3 (right) Capture Light/Shutterstock.com; p. 5 By O M 17/Shutterstock.com; p. 6 PM Images/Iconica/Getty Images; p. 9 Smit/Shutterstock.com; p. 10 dezi/Shutterstock.com; p. 13 (left) strelka/Shutterstock.com; p. 13 (collar) graphicphoto/iStock/Thinkstock, (bed) Luisa Leal Photography/Shutterstock.com, (brush) gvictoria/Shutterstock.com, (food and water bowls) exopixel/Shutterstock.com, (leash, toys) © iStockphoto.com/Liliboas; p. 14 Steve Bruckmann/Shutterstock.com; p. 17 Sergei Krasii/Shutterstock.com; p. 18 Nestor Rizhniak/Shutterstock.com; p. 19 Stockbyte/Thinkstock; p. 21 Nikol Mansfeld/Shutterstock.com.

Enslow Publishing

101 W. 23rd Street
Suite 240
New York, NY 10011
USA   enslow.com

CONTENTS

IS A JACK RUSSELL TERRIER RIGHT FOR YOU?

Jack Russell terriers make great pets. They enjoy homes with large yards where they can play. If your family is active, a Jack Russell terrier might be right for you.

Jack Russell terriers can have smooth, short coats or longer, rough coats.

A DOG OR A PUPPY?

Some Jack Russell terrier puppies are harder to train than others. If you do not have time to train a puppy, an older Jack Russell terrier may be better for your family.

Jack Russell terriers grow to be small in size.

Puppies left alone too long can become bored and get into trouble.

LOVING YOUR JACK RUSSELL TERRIER

This small dog with a big heart is easy to love.

They are brave, friendly, and playful.

Curled at your feet or chasing a ball, this dog likes being with its owner.

EXERCISE

Jack Russell terriers need lots of time to run, jump, and play. They are always ready for a game of **fetch** with a ball. Your Jack Russell terrier will enjoy walks on a **leash**.

Jack Russell terriers need a large fenced-in yard to play in.

FEEDING YOUR JACK RUSSELL TERRIER

Jack Russell terriers can be fed wet or dry dog food. Ask a veterinarian (vet), a doctor for animals, which food is best for your dog and how much to feed her.

Give your Jack Russell terrier fresh, clean water every day.

Remember to keep your dog's food and water dishes clean. Dirty dishes can make a dog sick.

Do not feed your dog people food. It can make her sick.

Your new dog will need:

a collar with a tag

a bed

a brush

food and water dishes

a leash

toys

GROOMING

Jack Russell terriers need to be brushed often because they **shed**. This means their hair falls out. Brushing your Jack Russell terrier will help keep him clean and looking his best.

Your dog will need a bath every so often. Use a gentle soap made just for dogs. A Jack Russell terrier's nails need to be clipped. A vet or **groomer** can show you how. Your dog's ears should be cleaned and her teeth should be brushed by an adult.

WHAT YOU SHOULD KNOW

Most Jack Russell terriers will dig and bark a lot.

Jack Russell terriers like to be with other Jack Russell terriers. They are not good with cats or small animals.

Jack Russell terriers have lots of energy. These high-energy dogs love spending time outside.

Because of their energy and barking, Jack Russell terriers are not dogs for apartment living.

You will need to take your new dog to the vet for a checkup. He will need shots, called vaccinations, and yearly checkups to keep him healthy. If you think your dog may be sick or hurt, call your vet.

A GOOD FRIEND

Like a good friend, your Jack Russell terrier will make you laugh for years to come.

Jack Russell terriers can live 15 years or more!

NOTE TO PARENTS

It is important to consider having your dog spayed or neutered when the dog is young. Spaying and neutering are operations that prevent unwanted puppies and can help improve the overall health of your dog.

It is also a good idea to microchip your dog, in case he or she gets lost. A vet will implant a microchip under the skin containing an identification number that can be scanned at a vet's office or animal shelter. The microchip registry is contacted and the company uses the ID number to look up your information from a database.

Some towns require licenses for dogs, so be sure to check with your town clerk.

For more information, speak with a vet.

There are many dogs, young and old, waiting to be adopted from animal shelters and rescue groups.

Words to Know

fetch To go after a toy and bring it back.

groomer A person who bathes and brushes dogs.

leash A chain or strap that attaches to the dog's collar.

shed When dog hair falls out so new hair can grow.

vaccinations Shots that dogs need to stay healthy.

veterinarian (vet) A doctor for animals.

22

Read About
Dogs

Books

Barnes, Nico. *Jack Russell Terriers*. Minneapolis, MN: Abdo Kids, 2014.

Medway, Jim. *Big Dogs, Little Dogs: A Visual Guide to the World's Dogs*. Richmond Hill, ON, Canada: Firefly Books, 2016.

Websites

American Canine Association Inc., Kids Corner
www.acakids.com
Visit the official website of the American Canine Association.

National Geographic for Kids, Pet Central
kids.nationalgeographic.com/explore/pet-central/
Learn more about dogs and other pets at the official site of the National Geographic Society for Kids.

INDEX

B
bark, 16
bathing, 15
brushing, 15

C
coat, 4

D
digging, 16
dishes, 12

E
ears, 15

F
fetch, 11
food, 12

G
groomer, 15

L
leash, 11
lifespan, 19
living space, 4, 16

M
microchip, 20

N
nails, 15

P
personality, 8, 16
playing, 11
puppies, 7

S
shed, 15
size, 7
spaying/neutering, 20

T
teeth, 15

V
vaccinations, 18
veterinarian (vet), 12, 15, 18, 20

W
water, 12